Günter Gerngross • Herbert Puchta

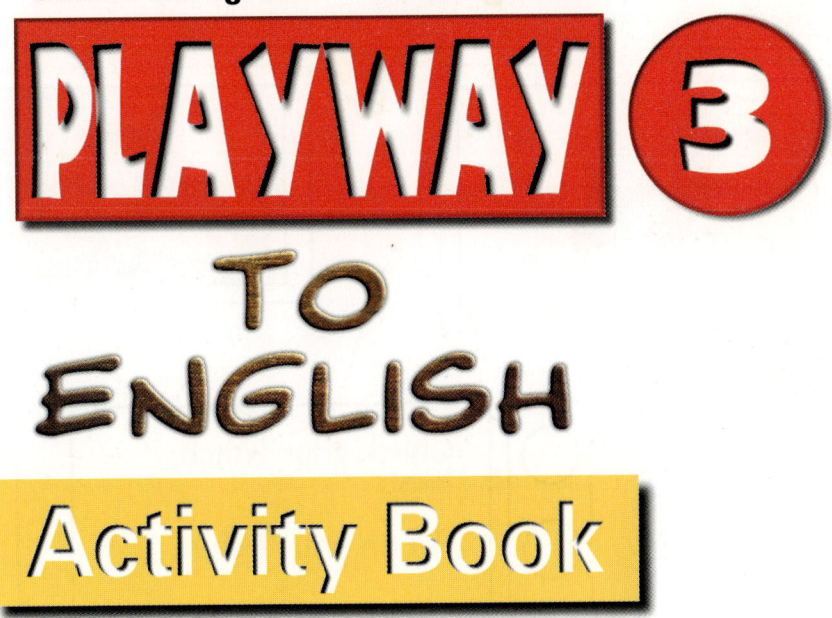

PLAYWAY 3
TO ENGLISH
Activity Book

Illustrations by Svjetlan Junakovi©

CAMBRIDGE
UNIVERSITY PRESS

Edition Helbling

Back to school

1 Listen and colour the circles. Then colour the frames of the pictures.

- ○ Check your watch.
- ○ Put on your T-shirt.
- ○ Get out of bed.
- ○ Wash your face.

- ○ Put your rubber in your pencil case.
- ○ Put your books in your schoolbag.
- ● Have a glass of milk.
- ○ Get your scissors.

2 **Listen and draw lines.**

Emma   Ken   Rosie   Richard

What has Emma got?

A red...

3 **Find the words.**

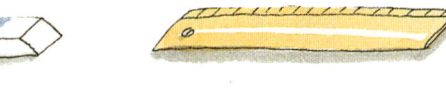

O	S	R	B	P	G	I	R	S
S	C	H	O	O	L	B	A	G
W	I	L	O	R	U	L	E	R
I	S	A	K	D	E	S	K	U
N	S	B	O	A	R	D	Y	E
D	O	E	Z	W	P	N	C	A
O	R	U	B	B	E	R	S	V
W	S	Y	P	E	N	C	I	L

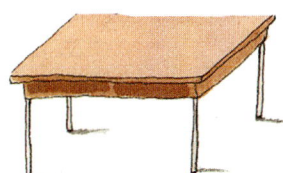
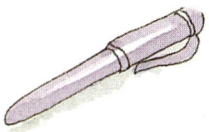

4 **Look, read and write the names.**

Alicia   Evan   Ann

Larry   Elissa   Will

His cap is blue. His shirt is orange. His jeans are blue and his shoes are grey.
His schoolbag is yellow and green.

What's his name?

_____

Her T-shirt is red. Her jeans are blue.
Her trainers are white and green.
Her schoolbag is blue and red.

What's her name?

_____

His cap is blue. His shirt is white and blue. His jeans and his shoes are grey.
His schoolbag is green.

What's his name?

_____

Her T-shirt is pink and white. Her jeans are blue. Her trainers are orange, grey and blue.
Her schoolbag is yellow.

What's her name?

_____

His cap is green. His shirt is orange and blue. His jeans are blue and his shoes are grey.
His schoolbag is red.

What's his name?

_____

Her T-shirt is red. Her jeans are blue.
Her trainers are white and grey.
Her schoolbag is blue.

What's her name?

_____

5 **Work in pairs.**

Ben

Sally

6 **Write the missing words.**

your face	your T-shirt	of bed	Put on	toast with jam
		your schoolbag		

Get out _____ . Wash _____ . Have some _____ .

_____ your jeans.   Put on _____ .   Get _____ .

5

Pets

1 **Do the puzzle. Then tick true or false.**

P	P	D	O	G	P	O	N	Y
O	H	M	O	U	S	E	M	I
N	A	S	P	I	D	E	R	B
Y	M	S	S	N	A	K	E	C
M	S	P	K	E	D	O	G	A
O	T	O	R	A	B	B	I	T
U	E	N	U	P	V	D	O	G
S	R	Y	N	I	C	A	T	N
E	B	U	D	G	I	E	L	R

	True	False
There are three dogs.		
There are two hamsters.		
There is one mouse.		
There are four guinea pigs.		
There is one spider.		
There are three ponies.		
There are two rabbits.		
There is one budgie.		
There are two cats.		
There is one snake.		

2 **Listen and stick in the animals. Find the hidden word.**

p. 41

1					
2					
3					

3 **Read and colour.**

The budgies are blue and green.

The guinea pig is orange, white and brown.

The rabbit is pink and grey.

The pony is black and white.

The snake is red and yellow.

4 **Fill in and cross out.**

two . onies

one mo . se

four h . msters

three . a . s

five r . bb . ts

seven gu . n . a p . gs

six . o . s

eight sp . d . . .

ten sn . . es

nine b . d . ies

7

5 **Follow the lines and write.**

Has Emma got a dog?   *Yes, she has.*

Has Alex got a snake?   *No, he hasn't.*

Has Joe got a mouse?

Has Eve got two guinea pigs?

Has Lisa got a pony?

Has Paul got a cat?

Has Ben got two rabbits?

Has Diana got a hamster?

Emma   Alex   Joe   Eve   Lisa   Paul   Ben   Diana

6 **Write the children's names. Then listen and check.**

Claire   Sonia   Tony   Barbara   Ken   Sidney

Who has got a mouse?   _____

Who has got a pony?   _____

Who has got a dog?   _____

Who has got a rabbit?   _____

Who has got a hamster?   _____

Who has got a cat?   _____

7 **Read Sally's and Bob's texts.**

I've got a cat. She is brown and white. She is two years old. Her name is Tipper.

Sally

My friend has got a rabbit. He is white and brown. He is three years old. His name is Flopsy.
I like Flopsy.

Bob

8 **Now write about your pet or your friend's pet.**

_____

_____

_____

_____

_____

_____

_____

Stick in a photo or draw a picture.

I'm scared

Unit 3

1 Tick the correct sentences.

He isn't scared of snakes.

He is scared of snakes.

He isn't scared of spiders.

He is scared of spiders.

She isn't scared of frogs.

She is scared of frogs.

He isn't scared of dogs.

He is scared of dogs.

They aren't scared of mice.

They are scared of mice.

They aren't scared of ghosts.

They are scared of ghosts.

2 Listen and fill in 😧 for scared and 🙂 for not scared.

Sheila	○	○	○	○	○	○
Alan	○	○	○	○	○	○
Nicola	○	○	○	○	○	○
Bill	○	○	○	○	○	○

11

3 **What are you scared of?**
Write the answers.

Are you scared of mice?   _____

Are you scared of ghosts?   _____

Are you scared of monsters?   _____

Are you scared of dogs?   _____

Are you scared of spiders?   _____

Are you scared of snakes?   _____

Are you scared of witches?   _____

Are you scared of skeletons?   _____

4 **Write your own text. Draw a picture.**

I'm not scared of mice.   *I'm* _____

I'm not scared of dogs.   _____

I'm not scared of snakes   _____

and I'm not scared of spiders,   _____

but I'm scared of the monster   *but I'm* _____

under my bed.   _____

5 **Fill in the words from the box. Then listen and check.**

goes away	sees	climbs	garden	runs away
is scared	dog	looks	down the tree	is

Max and the dog.

Max is in his neighbour's _____ .

He _____ a _____ .

The dog _____ at Max.

Max _____

He _____ .

He _____ a tree.

Max _____ very scared.

The dog _____ .

Max climbs _____ _____ .

Unit 4

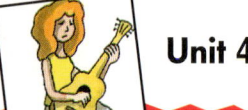

Feelings

1 **Match the words with the faces.**

happy
scared
angry
sad
tired

______ ______ ______ ______ ______

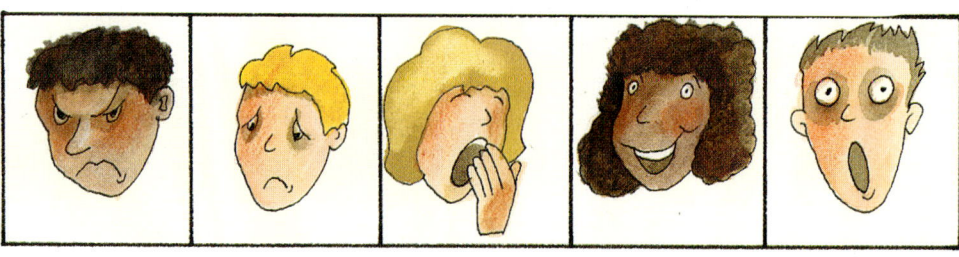

2 **Circle the words in the right colour.**

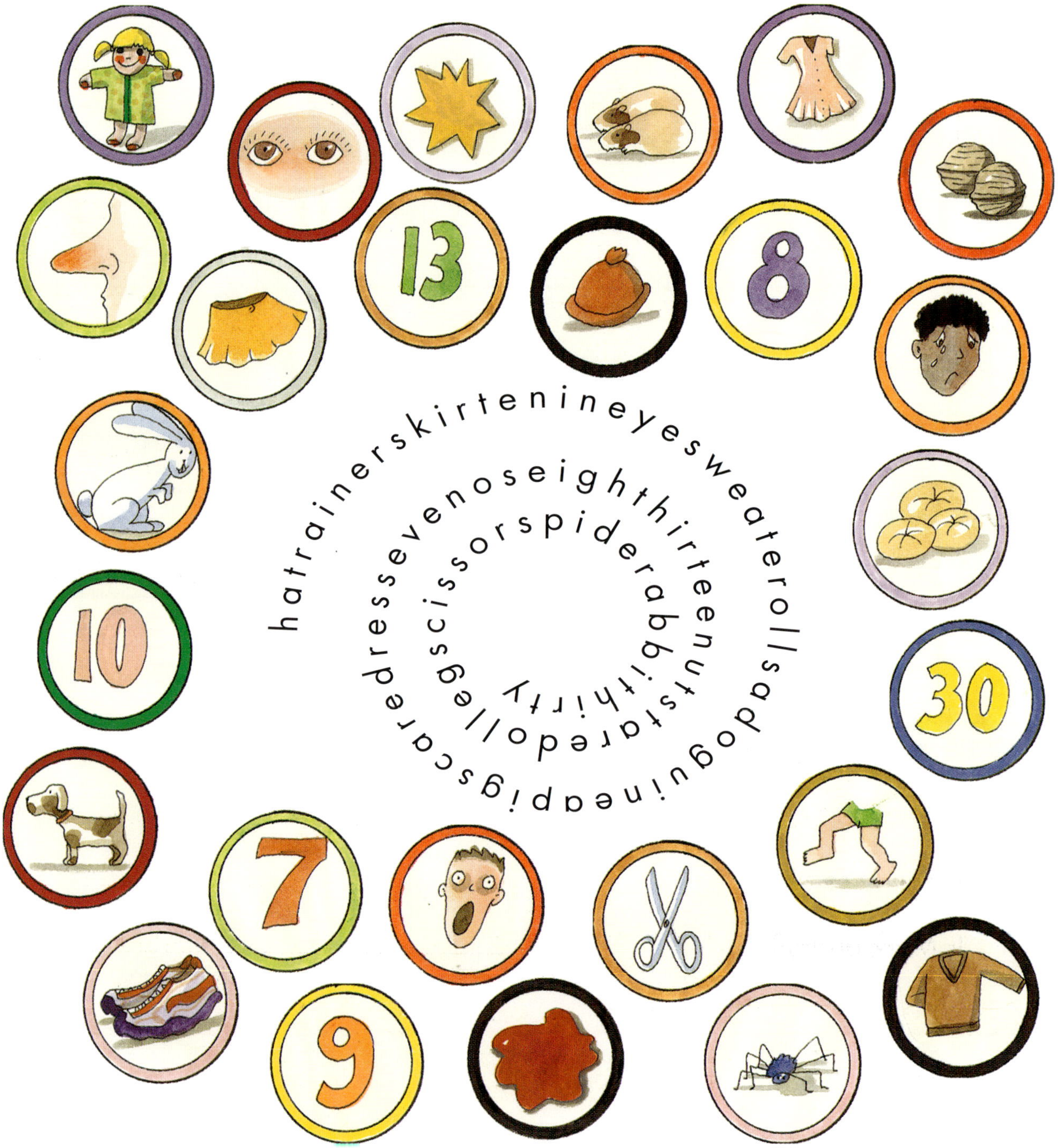

13
8
10
30
7
9
hatrainerskirtenineyesweaterollsadogguineapigscaredressevenoseighthirteenutstaredpollegscissorspiderabbithirty

3 **Guess the answers. Put the puzzle together and check**

p. 41

No, she isn't. Yes, they are. No, he isn't. Yes, he is. Yes, she is. No, they aren't.

Are Pam and Sue happy? _____

Is Peter tired? _____

Is Emma sad? _____

Is Mark angry? _____

Are Chris and Diana scared? _____

Is Laura angry? _____

Unit 4

4 **Listen and tick.**

1. Peter and Mark are
- ☐ tired.
- ☐ scared.
- ☐ angry.

2. Jeff is
- ☐ sad.
- ☐ angry.
- ☐ happy.

3. Emma is
- ☐ happy.
- ☐ scared.
- ☐ tired.

4. Sarah is
- ☐ tired.
- ☐ angry.
- ☐ sad.

5. Ben is
- ☐ angry.
- ☐ scared.
- ☐ sad.

6. Ann and Kathy are
- ☐ angry.
- ☐ happy.
- ☐ sad.

5 **Max's sunglasses. Fill in numbers. Then listen and check.**

6 **Cut out the answers and stick them in.
Then listen and check.**

 p. 43

Who is the best singer?

Where are we going?

Can you play tennis?

Have you got a pet, Sue?

A sheep's heart, please.

Here are your favourite
chocolates.

How old is your cat?

What colour is your budgie?

What's your name?

Where's the cinema?

1 Look at the puzzle pieces on page 43 for one minute. Then answer the questions below. Use the sentences in the box.

Yes, there is.	No, there isn't.	Yes, there are.	No, there aren't.

Is there a green door in the classroom?   _____

Are there six desks?   _____

Are there fourteen chairs?   _____

Is there a television?   _____

Is there a washbasin?   _____

Are there three windows?   _____

Is there a pot plant?   _____

Are there two brown cupboards?   _____

2 Cut out the puzzle pictures .
Stick them in and check your answers.

p. 43

3 **Can you find the words?**

A	B	C	D	E	G	H	I	K	L

M	N	O	P	R	S	T	U	X

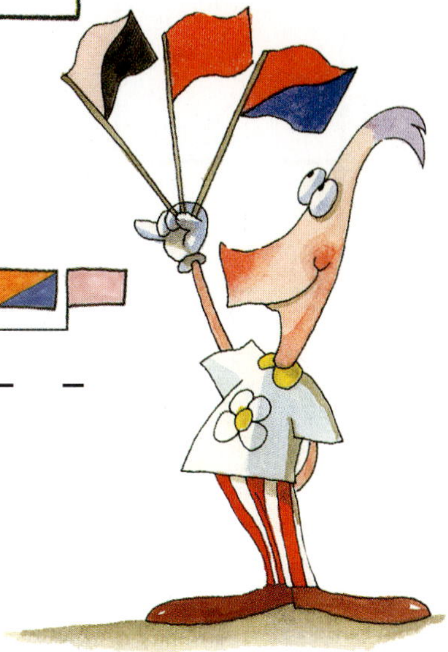

Where is the church?

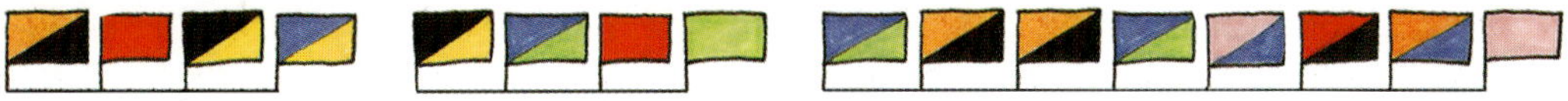

It's in _ _ _ _ _ _ _ , _ _ _ _ _ _ _ _ _ _ _

_ _ _ _ _ _ _ _ .

Where is the hospital?

It's _ _ _ _ _ _ _ _ _ _ _ _ _ .

Where is the cinema?

It's _ _ _ _ _ _ _ _ _ _ .

Where is the supermarket?

It's _ _ _ _ _ _ _ _ _ _ _ .

Where is the post office?

It's _ _ _ _ _ _ _ _ _ _ _

_ _ _ _ _ _ _ _ _ _ .

4 **Now complete the map.**

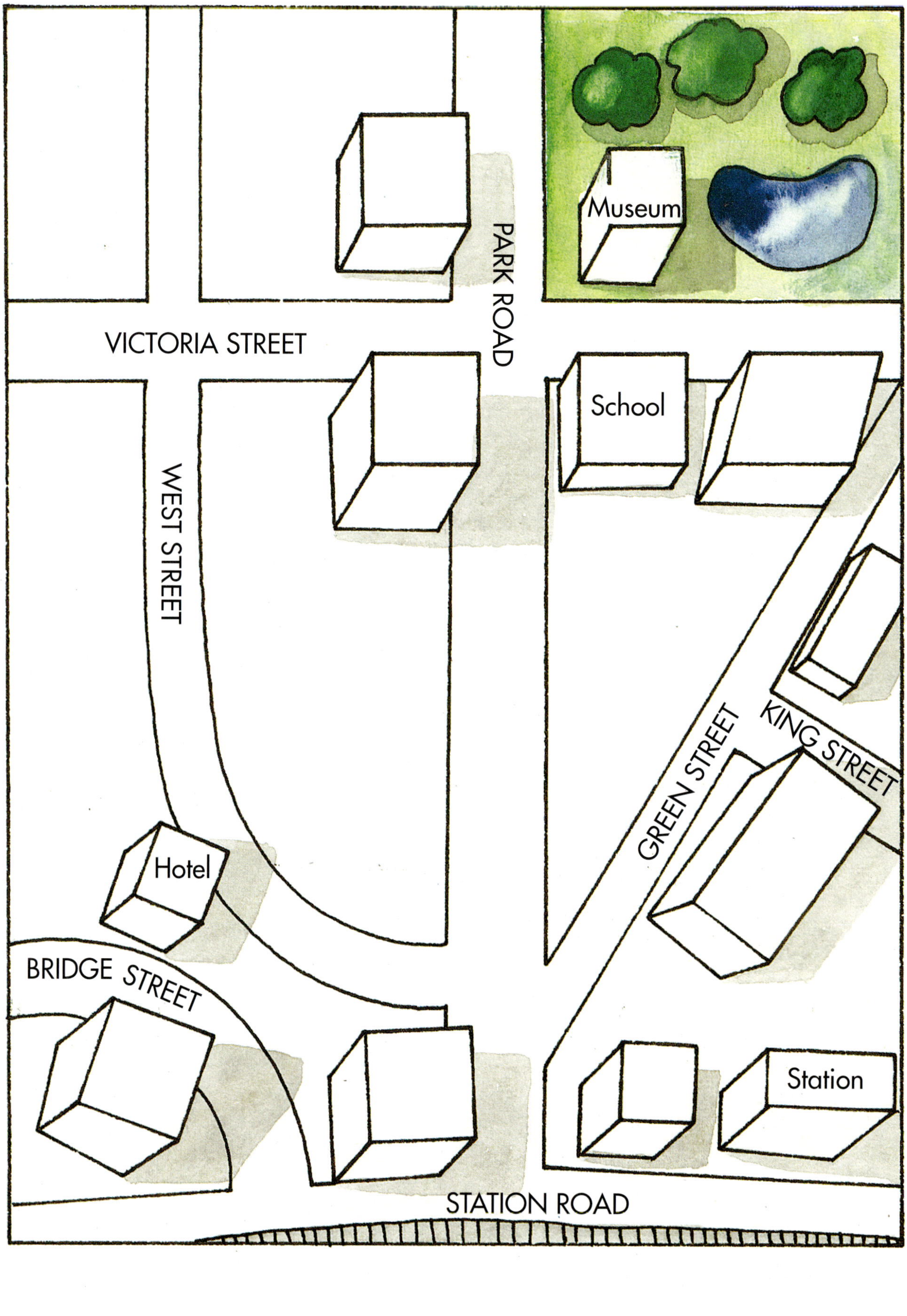

VICTORIA STREET

PARK ROAD

Museum

School

WEST STREET

GREEN STREET

KING STREET

Hotel

BRIDGE STREET

Station

STATION ROAD

5 **Look and complete the dialogues.**

1

Tourist: Excuse me, where's the post office?

Man: It's_____ the station.

2

Tourist: _____ me, where's the _____?

Woman: It's in the park.

3

Tourist: Excuse me,_____ the hospital?

Man: It's_____ _____ the school.

4

Tourist: _____ me, _____ the church?

Woman: It's_____ Park Road.

5

Tourist: _____ me, _____ the hotel.

Man: It's_____ _____ supermarket.

6 **Now listen and check.**

21

Free time

1 **Cut out the answers and stick them in. Then listen and check.**

 p. 47

Can you cook spaghetti?

What colour is your new sweater?

How old is your brother?

Excuse me, where is the station?

Where are you going?

Are you scared of dogs?

Excuse me, where is the museum?

Who is this boy?

2 **Cut out the words and pictures. Create a funny text.**
Colour the black and white pictures.

p. 45

My name is
William Pinky.

I can't ,

I can't ,

I can't .

But I can .

Unit 6

3 **Listen and stick in the pictures. Then stick in the words.**

 p. 47

On Monday he

On Tuesday he

On Wednesday he

On Thursday he

On Friday he

On Saturday he

And on Sunday he rests.

4 Play the game with a friend. You need two dice .
Throw the dice and complete the words.

2 = A	7 = R
3 = E	8 = S
4 = F	9 = U
5 = H	10 = D
6 = I	11 = Y

12 = Miss a turn

MONDAY

| M | O | N | | | |

TUESDAY

| T | | | | | |

WEDNESDAY

| W | | | N | | | | |

THURSDAY

| T | | | | | | | |

FRIDAY

| | | | | | |

SATURDAY

| | | T | | | | |

SUNDAY

| | | N | | | |

Head and shoulders

1 **Find the words.**

```
        [ S ] 
            E
    T       [ ] H
        U
            G
H       [ S ]
        [ Y ]   S
        [ S ]
    O   [ S ]
```

2 **Listen. Complete the text about the monkey. Colour the picture.**

His_____is yellow. His_____ear is green, and his right_____is red. His_____are blue and his nose is_____. His_____is red.

His_____arm is_____and his right _____is pink. His hands are_____. His _____leg is grey, and his left leg is _____. His_____are yellow.

blue
left
hair
mouth
right
eyes
pink
feet
left
orange
arm
ear
green

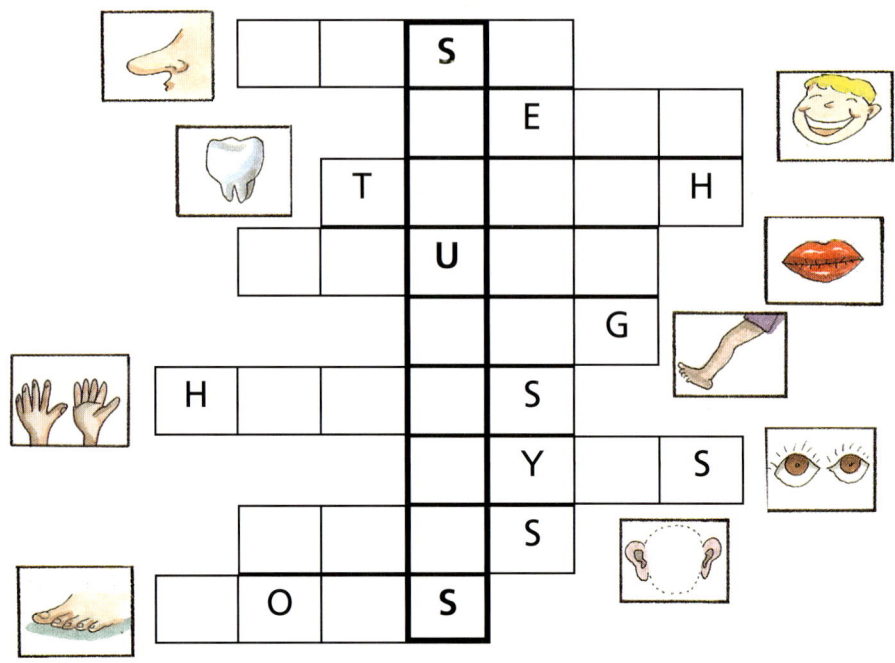

3 Complete the text. Listen and check.

This is Bozo.

His hair is_____. His left ear is _____and his right ear is_____.
His eyes are_____and his nose is _____. His mouth is_____.
His left arm is_____and his right arm is_____. His hands are_____.
His right leg is_____and his left leg is_____. His feet are_____.

4 Colour the picture. Then complete the text and read it out.

This is Bozo's friend Pippa.

Her hair is_____. Her left ear is _____and her right ear is_____
_____. Her eyes are_____and her nose is _____. Her mouth is
_____.

Her left arm is_____ and her right arm is_____. Her hands are_____.
Her right leg is_____and her left leg is_____. Her feet are_____.

5 Listen and point.

6 Play the game with a friend. You need a dice.

7 **Read the sentences. Tick true or false.**

T   F

1. The man with the brown eyes and the big nose has got a small mouth.
2. The woman with the blue eyes and the wide mouth has got long, red hair.
3. The woman with the blue eyes and the small mouth has got a big nose.
4. The woman with the long, brown hair has got a small mouth and a small nose.
5. The man with the long, black hair has got grey eyes and a small mouth.
6. The woman with the brown eyes and the big ears has got a big nose.
7. The man with the blue eyes has got a big nose and long, fair hair.
8. The woman with the green eyes has got short, fair hair and a small mouth.
9. The man with the short, black hair has got big ears and a big nose.
10. The man with the brown eyes and the short, grey hair has got a small nose.

What's the time?

1 **Colour the frames.**

| It's ten o'clock. | It's quarter past three. | It's quarter to six. |

| It's half past two. | It's quarter to twelve. | It's quarter past five. |

2 **The missing flowers. Fill in numbers. Listen and check.**

Linda, Benny, Max, dinner's ready.

Look at the flowers, Linda!

Oh, no.

Max, we are angry with you.

?

I'm sorry, Max.

Me too.

It's alright.

Oh, look at the flowers, Benny.

Max, come here!

3 **Find Linda, Christine and Sally. Write their names.**

Linda gets up at seven o'clock. She has breakfast at half past seven.
She goes to school at eight o'clock. She comes home at half past three.
She goes to bed at quarter to nine.

Christine gets up at eight. She has breakfast at quarter past eight.
She goes to school at half past eight. She comes home at four.
She goes to bed at half past nine.

Sally gets up at seven o'clock. She has breakfast at half past seven.
She goes to school at quarter to eight. She comes home at three.
She goes to bed at nine.

Unit 8

4 **Cut out the clocks . Listen and stick them in.**

p. 47

I get up at _____ . I have my breakfast at _____ .

I go to school at _____ . School starts at _____ and

finishes at _____ . From _____ to _____ I play

with my friends. I go to bed at _____ .

This is me at _____ .

5 **Write your own text.**

6 Listen and fill in the numbers.

Unit 9

Buying things

1 **Read the crazy sentences. Guess the answers.**
Put the puzzle together and check.

 p. 49

	True	False
Five pink tomatoes are making woolly hats.		
Three blue ducks are standing on their heads.		
Four red pencil cases are playing tennis.		
Three yellow ladybirds are blowing blue bubbles.		
One orange pear is eating spaghetti.		
Four green clocks are playing cards.		

2 Write a crazy sentence and draw the picture.

3 An umbrella for Max. Fill in the numbers. Listen and check.

Unit 9

4 Stick in the sentences.

p. 51

5 **Put the sentences in the correct order. Then listen and check.**

[ ] How much are the white and pink trainers?

[ ] OK. And a pair of white socks.

[ ] Here you are.

[1] Good morning.

[ ] The white and pink trainers and a pair of white socks. That's £27, please.

[ ] £25.

[ ] Good morning.

[ ] Thank you.

6 Fill in [is] or [are] .

How much		the jeans?	£26.
How much		the cap?	£3.
How much		the T-shirt?	£6.
How much		the sweater?	£47.
How much		the socks?	£4.
How much		the shoes?	£19.

Tammy, the queen of jams

1 Stick in the words.

 p. 51

2 **Listen and check.**

END OF THE YEAR QUIZ

1. What's the name of the new girl in Linda and Benny's class?

2. Ted takes Snow White to the

3. Ted buys a

4. The queen brings Snow White

5. Max is scared of the neighbour's

6. The ladybirds are looking for the

7. Lizzie can play the

8. This is what Lizzie cooks for her friends:

9. Who has a broken leg and comes to see Dr Kangaroo?

10. The animals play football, darts and

11. The farmer wakes up at

12. Max drinks Benny's

3 **Write about yourself.**

My favourite colour is _____.

My favourite day is _____.

My favourite sport is _____.

My favourite pet is a _____.

My favourite number is _____.

I can't _____.

I'm scared of _____ .

I'm not scared of _____ .

I like _____.

I don't like _____ .

The colour of my eyes: _____ .

The colour of my hair: _____ .

My best friend's name is _____ .

Unit 2

Unit 4

Unit 4,6 - p. 17

To the airport.	Thank you.
Here you are. Two pounds, please.	Snow White.
Green and yellow.	Yes, I can.
Five.	Yes, I have.
Lucy.	

Unit 5

Unit 5,2 - p. 18

Unit 6

Unit 6,2 - p. 23

sing

cook spaghetti

dance

ride a bike

play football

ride a horse

roller-blade

sail a boat

play the guitar

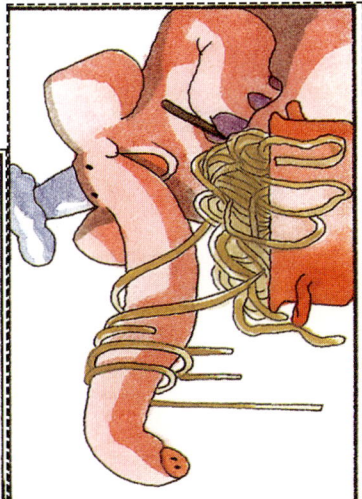

Unit 6,1 - p. 22

To the station.	Yes, I am.
Red and yellow.	It's opposite the church.
He is six.	The station is next to the post office.
Yes, I can.	He is new in our class. His name is Ben.

Unit 6,3 - p. 24

plays volleyball.	rides his horse.	swims in the river.
plays football.	rides his bike.	plays tennis.

Unit 8

Unit 8,4 - p. 32

Unit 9,1 - p. 34

Unit 9,4 - p. 36

1

| Here you are. | That's £3. | Bye! | Bye! | Thank you. | A blue cap, plaese. |

2

| How much is the sweater? | OK. The sweater and the red T-shirt, please. | Yes, it's nice. | £17. | A red T-shirt and a sweater. That's £21. |

| Do you like it, Sue? | Yes, the T-shirt is for me. | A red T-shirt? |

Unit 10,1 - p. 38

angry		tree	ears
	black	boat	apple
blue		flower	horse
cat	ghost		snake
	dog	green	tooth
	heart	chair	thirteen
door		mouth	yellow
seventy	sixty-five		leg
	eyes	spider	window
	mirror	key	socks
scared		thirty-four	tired
rabbit			

Make decorations for your classroom.

You need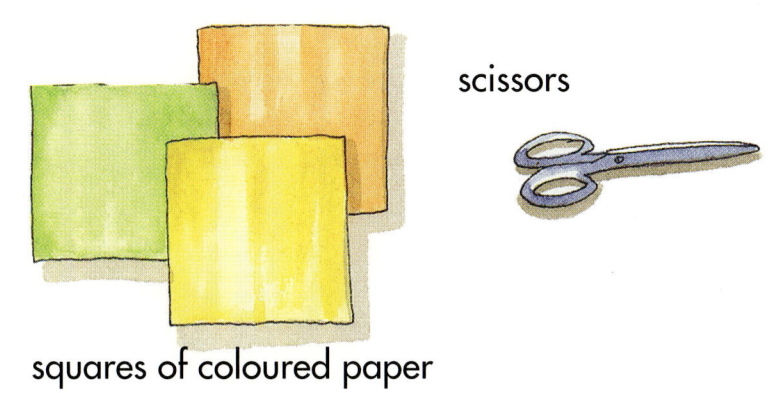

scissors

squares of coloured paper

1 Fold the square like this.

2 Then fold it like this.

3 Hold it like this.

4 Fold it again.

5 Cut here - - - - - - -.

6

Decorate the windows of your classroom.